www.dk.com

Project Editor Sheila Hanly
Senior Art Editor Rowena Alsey

Senior Editor Nicola Tuxworth
Managing Editor Jane Yorke
Managing Art Editor Chris Scollen
Production Marguerite Fenn and Catherine Semark

Photography Steve Shott and Susanna Price
Illustrations Robin Jacques and Graham Philpot

Language consultant Professor Elizabeth Goodacre
Natural History consultant Steve Parker
Medical consultant Dr T Kramer
Geography consultant James Mills-Hicks, DK Cartography

First published in Great Britain in 1993
by Dorling Kindersley Limited,
9 Henrietta Street, London, WC2E 8PS

Copyright © 1993, 1999 Dorling Kindersley Limited, London
Reprinted 1994, 1995 (twice), 1996 (twice), 1997, 1998, 1999
Photography (page 44 dog, sheep, goats; page 56 camel;
page 58 zebra; page 60 jaguar; page 65 penguin;
front cover sheep) copyright ©1991 Philip Dowell

A CIP catalogue record for this book is
available from the British Library

ISBN 0-7513-6305-7

Colour reproduction by J. Film Process Singapore Pte., Ltd.
Printed and bound in Italy by L.E.G.O.

DK First Encyclopedia

Carol Watson

LONDON • NEW YORK • SYDNEY • DELHI

Note to parents and teachers

One of the most amazing things about young children is their fascination with the world around them, embodied in the questions they ask. **DK First Encyclopedia** has been specially designed to answer some of those questions and to introduce children to the exciting world of books as a source of information about themselves and their world.

A first book of knowledge

DK First Encyclopedia is arranged in themes that parallel a child's developing curiosity and interests. Starting with a child's immediate daily experiences, the themes extend to an exploration of the wider world, covering such topics as animals, climatic regions, the people of the world, and even outer space. By reading through the themes in order, you can encourage children to make connections between their own lives and those of people living in other parts of the world.

Looking at pictures

The encyclopedia is packed with stunning full-colour photographs that let children see what animals and objects really look like and arouse their interest to know more about them. Detailed drawings show the context in which things are found, and imaginative picture sequences reveal some of the processes that occur both in the natural and the human world. When sharing the book with younger children, you can read the text aloud, using the photographs and drawings as starting points for further discussion. It would be useful to point out to children the conventions of illustration and make sure that they understand that not all the objects on the page are shown in scale.

Reading aloud

Many children have stories read aloud to them, but this is not necessarily the case with information books. As a result, beginner readers are often unfamiliar with the written style used in such books and less competent in predicting what the text will "say" – a key step in learning to read. The pages dealing with children's everyday experiences are addressed to the reader, but the more impersonal, instructional style of information books is also introduced. Older children, who are starting to read on their own, will find the clear, simple text easy to follow. The familiar word is always used to name an object or animals, followed by the more specific or technical term. This helps young children to read and understand the information easily, and to increase their vocabulary at the same time.

Finding information

DK First Encyclopedia is designed to prepare children for more complicated information books. A complete alphabetical index is included to simplify the task of locating information on specific topics. You can also encourage children to use the index for cross-referencing. A pronunciation guide for more difficult words has been included with the index. It can be used to help to expand children's spoken vocabulary and may also be useful to adults when reading aloud.

A book to grow up with

In sharing and enjoying this book with your children, you will introduce them to an exciting world of information and knowledge that will be invaluable to them throughout their lives.

Elizabeth Goodacre
Language Consultant

Contents

The human body

The human body is made up of different parts, each with a special job to do. All the parts work together so that you can move, breathe, grow, and stay alive.

Skin
Your body is covered all over by layers of skin. The skin protects the inside of your body and stops germs from getting in.

Muscles are attached to your skeleton under your skin. You use your muscles for lifting, carrying, and moving around.

hand

Arms and legs
You lift and carry things with your arms and hands. You use your legs and feet to walk and run.

head

arm

Bones are connected by joints so that people can move and bend.

chest

skull

elbow joint

hip bone

rib cage

Inside the body
Inside your body are soft parts called organs that do different jobs.

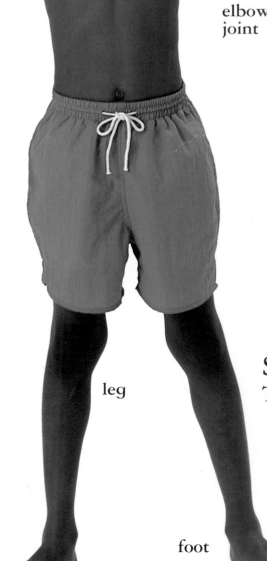

The brain inside your head controls all your thoughts and movements.

The lungs in your chest breathe in fresh air and take in the oxygen you need to stay alive.

The heart is a muscle that pumps blood around your body to give it oxygen and food.

The stomach is where the food you eat starts to be broken down. Food gives the body energy and helps it to grow.

knee joint

leg

Skeleton
The human skeleton is a frame made of 206 bones. It supports the soft parts of the body.

foot

Boys and girls

You are either a boy or a girl. A boy is male and grows up to be a man. A girl is female and grows up to be a woman.

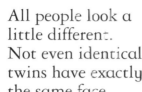

All people look a little different. Not even identical twins have exactly the same face.

Growing up

People grow from the moment their lives begin. As they grow, their bodies change. People usually stop growing when they are about 20 years old, but their bodies do not stop changing.

Speech

The vocal cords in your throat make sounds. With your mouth and tongue you can shape the sounds into words so that you can speak to other people.

Hearing

You hear with your ears. They collect sounds from the air and send them to your brain. Your brain then tells you what the sounds mean.

Sight

People use their eyes to see. Eyes act like cameras, sending pictures to the brain. Some people need to wear glasses to see clearly.

Taste

Your tongue helps you to taste. It is covered with taste buds that can tell if something is sweet or sour, salty or bitter.

Touch

When you touch something, nerves in your skin send messages to your brain. Your brain can tell whether the thing is soft or hard, rough or smooth, hot or cold.

Smell

You smell with your nose. Nerves in your nose send messages to your brain, which tells you what you are smelling.

Families

A family is all the people you are related to. Everyone is part of a family, whether it is large or small. Many families get together to celebrate special events.

Grandparents

Your grandparents are your mother and father's parents. You are their grandchild.

Some children call their grandmother, "Granny" and their grandfather, "Grandpa".

Parents

Your mother and father are your parents. If you are a girl, you are your parents' daughter. If you are a boy, you are your parents' son.

Aunt

If your mother or father has a sister, she is your aunt.

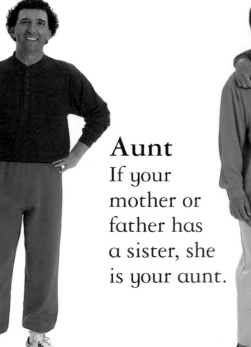

Some children call their mother and father, "Mummy" and "Daddy".

Uncle

If your mother or father has a brother, he is your uncle.

Cousin

If your aunt and uncle have children, they are your cousins.

Your aunt's husband is also your uncle.

Sister and brother

If your parents have another child who is a girl, she is your sister. If your parents have another child who is a boy, he is your brother.

These children were born on the same day. They are twins.

A new baby

This family has a new member – a baby girl. Everyone is looking forward to helping to take care of her.

A family holiday

Many families enjoy holidays together. This little girl is going to the country with her father. They will be able to spend lots of time with each other.

Visiting Granny and Grandpa

A visit to your grandparents can be a special treat. Some children's grandparents live at home with them.

Getting married

When two people get married, they become part of a new family. Their families may get together to celebrate the day. They wear their best clothes and take lots of photographs.

Some people have videos made of their wedding so that they can watch and enjoy it all over again.

People often give one another brightly wrapped presents on their birthday.

A birthday

Every year, each of us has a special day – a birthday. Some people have a party on their birthday. They invite their family and friends to share the day with them.

Houses and homes

People live in different kinds of home. Many people live in a house or flat in one place. People called nomads move around, living in tents or caravans. Some homes are large with lots of rooms with different uses, others are smaller with one or two rooms.

Caravan

A caravan is a house that can move. This large caravan, or trailer, usually stays in one place. Some caravans have wheels and can be towed by a car.

Living room

A living or sitting room is a comfortable room where people can relax, read, or watch television.

People may decorate the rooms of their home in the colours they like best.

Kitchen

People use a kitchen to store, prepare, and cook their food. Most modern homes have gas or electric cookers for cooking food. Some people eat their meals in the kitchen.

Types of home

Homes come in lots of different shapes and sizes – from houses and cottages built with wood, bricks, or stone, to modern flats or apartments made of glass and concrete.

On the outskirts of a city, there is usually more space to build individual houses than in the crowded city centre.

wooden house

brick house

villa

Stilts help to keep a house level when it is built on a steep hillside.

House on stilts

People who live near rivers and marshes often build their homes on stilts. The stilts keep the house high up off the ground, making it safe from floods.

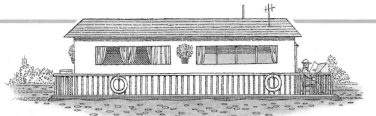

Houseboat

A houseboat is a home that floats on water. Some people live on their houseboats all the time. Others use them as holiday homes.

Bathroom

There is usually a bath or shower, a washbasin, and a lavatory in a bathroom. People use a bathroom for washing, shaving, and cleaning their teeth.

Bedroom

A bedroom is a room in which people can relax and sleep. People also get dressed and keep clothes in a bedroom. Many children spend time in their bedroom, playing with toys or reading books.

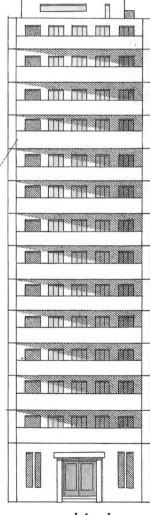

Tower blocks are made up of many small homes, called flats, built on top of one another. They are built in crowded cities.

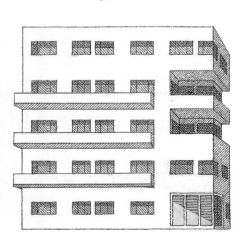

apartment block

terraced houses

tower block

13

Pets

Many people keep tame animals as pets. Pets are fun to play with and care for, but looking after them is hard work. Everyone in the family should agree about getting a pet.

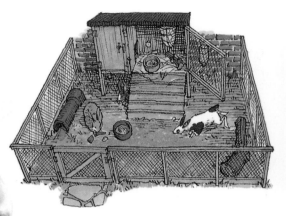

Mouse

A tiny pet mouse should be handled carefully. Mice need a big cage to live in. The cage must be cleaned out two or three times each week.

Pony

Some children are lucky enough to be able to learn to ride a pony. A pony should be groomed and exercised every day.

Rabbit

Rabbits are friendly animals. If you play with them often they quickly become tame. Rabbits need to live out-of-doors in a hutch with a fenced area to run about in.

Some budgies learn to copy your voice and say different words.

Fish

Fish are fascinating to watch as they swim around in a big glass tank called an aquarium. These goldfish need to be fed a small amount of food every day.

Budgerigar

A budgerigar, or budgie, is a colourful bird. The best place to keep budgies is in the garden in a big cage called an aviary.

Dog

A dog is a good friend and likes lots of love and attention. Dogs need exercise every day to keep them healthy. They enjoy long walks and chasing sticks and balls.

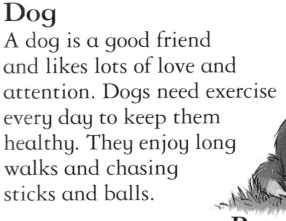

Pet care

All pets need to be kept clean. A dog's coat should be gently brushed to get rid of loose hair and dirt.

Guinea pig

Guinea pigs are shy animals, but are easy to tame. They like to eat a lot and need plenty of exercise.

Visiting the vet

A sick pet

If your pet is sick, stops eating, or drinks more than usual, it should be taken to the vet for a check-up.

Check-up

The vet will look carefully at your pet for signs of illness and might give it an injection.

Medicine

Your pet may need pills or special food to help it get better. It might have to stay at the vet's overnight.

Cat

Cats enjoy playing and being stroked. But they also need time on their own. After a meal, a cat will spend a long time washing itself carefully. Cats sleep most of the day and are usually more active at night.

All in one day

A day starts in the morning, when the sun rises. During the daylight hours, people are busy – working, eating, and playing. By night-time, when the sun sets, most people are tired and ready to rest.

Morning

In the morning, it is time to wake up, get dressed, and get ready for the day ahead.

Breakfast

Breakfast is the first meal of the day. It gives people energy to keep going all morning.

Off to school

On weekdays, most children go to school. They get to school by walking, riding a bicycle, or travelling in a bus or car.

Time to learn

During the school day, children learn things such as reading, writing, science, and mathematics. They can make friends and learn to work together.

At some schools, children spend time painting and drawing every day. It is a good way to learn about colours, patterns, and shapes.

Teachers help children to learn and show them how to find things out for themselves.

Children do different things during the school day. They might spend some time singing and making music together.

Many children enjoy playing ball games in the park.

Afternoon

In the afternoon, when school is over, there is often time to play. Children can play outside or indoors – reading books, drawing, using the computer, or watching television.

Mealtime

In the evening, many families share a meal. It can be a time when they tell one another what they have done during the day.

Some families eat their main meal around midday instead of in the evening.

Evening

In the evening, it begins to get dark as the sun goes down. Most people need to rest and relax after a busy day. Some children read a story before bedtime.

Time for bed

At night, most people are tired. It feels good to go to bed and sleep until morning.

Bathtime

It is important to keep your body clean and fresh by washing carefully every day.

17

Games and sports

People of all ages enjoy playing games and sports. We play sports for fun and to relax, or for exercise to keep us fit and healthy. Some sports and games are played by people on their own, others are played by many people in groups called teams.

Cycling

Many people enjoy riding a bicycle along country roads with their family or a group of friends. Cycling is good exercise and can be an exciting sport. Cyclists can race one another on cycling tracks.

Ice skating

Ice skaters wear special boots with a thin blade fixed to the sole of the boot. These help them to glide over the ice. People can go to ice rinks to skate on ice that is smooth and safe.

Judo

Judo is a sport for two players. They wear white judo suits and stand on a soft mat. The players learn special movements to throw each other on to the floor.

Gymnastics

A person who does gymnastics is called a gymnast. A gymnast must be strong and supple to jump, turn somersaults, balance, twist, and cartwheel. This gymnast is wearing a stretchy leotard so that she can move easily.

Swimming

Swimming is a sport that people can enjoy in teams or by themselves. They can race up and down a swimming pool, or have fun, splashing and playing with friends.

Running

Many people enjoy running in races. They run on roads, on athletics tracks, or across the countryside.

Runners wear special shoes with thick, soft soles to protect and support their feet.

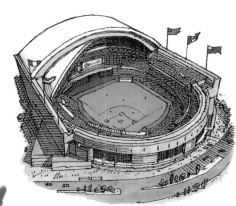

Watching sports

Large sports stadiums are built in many cities. People go to stadiums to watch their favourite sports team in action.

Basketball

Basketball is played by two teams of ten players each. Five players from each team work together to score points. A team scores points when a player throws the ball into the net, or basket.

Wearing a sports outfit, such as shorts and a singlet, helps players to keep cool and move freely.

Inline skating

Inline skaters speed along on wheels attached to special boots. They wear a helmet and elbow, knee, and wrist pads for protection in case they fall.

Ball games

Many sports are played with a ball. Football players kick a ball between two goal-posts to score points. American football players can pick up and throw the ball. Tennis players use a racquet to hit the ball over a net. Baseball players use a long bat to hit the ball.

football

tennis ball

American football

baseball

19

Keeping healthy

We would all like to be healthy. To help us to stay fit and strong, we should try to look after our bodies by keeping clean, eating well, exercising, and getting enough sleep.

Sleeping
Sleeping gives our bodies and minds a chance to rest. Children need more sleep than adults.

Keeping clean
To stay healthy, we need to keep our bodies clean. We should wash all over at least once a day.

flannel

nailbrush

soap

toothbrush and toothpaste

shampoo

Nails
Dirt collects under our fingernails. We should trim them neatly and make sure that they are scrubbed clean.

Teeth
When children are about six or seven, their baby teeth fall out. A new set of teeth grows. We must look after our teeth properly by brushing them every morning and night, and by not eating too many sweets.

Visiting the dentist
We need to visit the dentist at least twice a year. The dentist checks our teeth and gums to make sure that they are healthy and strong.

If your tooth has a hole in it, the dentist will fill it.

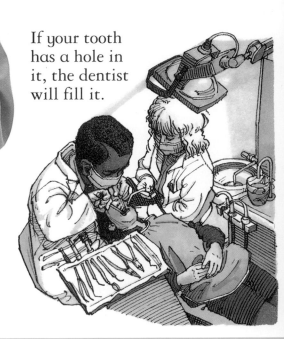

Hair
You can keep your hair clean and shiny by washing it often. Brushing and combing your hair gets rid of tangles.

20

Diet

It is important to drink lots of water every day and to eat plenty of fresh fruit and vegetables.

Exercise

We can keep our bodies fit and healthy by exercising often. Exercise makes our muscles stronger. Running and playing ball games or other sports are all good ways of keeping fit.

Skipping out-of-doors is a fun way of keeping fit and strong.

First aid

If we cut ourselves, we must act quickly to stop the cut from getting infected. This is called first aid. The cut must be cleaned with warm water and antiseptic and covered with a plaster to keep it clean.

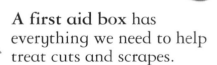

A first aid box has everything we need to help treat cuts and scrapes.

Visiting the doctor

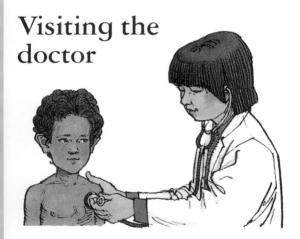

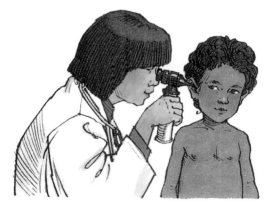

Check-up

The doctor listens to your heart and lungs with a stethoscope to check that they are working properly.

Examination

The doctor looks inside your ears, mouth, and eyes to see if you are healthy or to find out if anything is wrong.

Injections

You might need special injections to stop you from catching serious diseases or to make you better when ill.

pasta shapes   spaghetti

Pasta

Pasta is made from flour and eggs, rolled out and cut into many different shapes. After being cooked, pasta is often eaten with a sauce.

Food we eat

People need to eat every day. Food helps us to grow, gives us energy, and keeps us strong and healthy. We get food from animals and plants and turn it into different meals. Some food can be eaten raw, but other food tastes better when it is cooked.

Cereal

A bowl of cereal and milk for breakfast gives us energy first thing in the morning.

cheese   bread

lettuce   tomato

Rice

Many people eat rice as their main food. Rice is eaten on its own, or with vegetables, fish, or meat.

Bread

Bread is an important food in most countries of the world. Many people eat bread as a sandwich. They take two or more slices of bread and put a filling, such as cheese, between them.

Baking bread

Mixing

To make bread, you mix together flour, yeast, and water. These form a soft paste called dough.

Baking

The bread dough is pressed into a loaf-shaped baking tin. The tin is put into a hot oven for the loaf to bake.

Eating

Once the loaf is baked, it is taken out of the oven and left to cool. The bread can be sliced up and eaten.

Egg

Eggs can be eaten poached, scrambled, fried, or boiled. We also use raw eggs in recipes to make things such as pastry, cakes, and sauces.

boiled egg

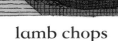

tinned sardines   lamb chops   chicken

Fish and meat

Fish and meat give us protein, which helps our bodies to grow. Most fish and meat needs to be cooked before we can eat it. Vegetarians are people who choose not to eat fish or meat.

Vegetables

Vegetables are full of vitamins that help to keep us healthy. Many people enjoy eating cooked vegetables with a hot meal, or raw vegetables in a salad.

This hot baked potato is filled with grated cheese.

orange juice

hot chocolate

Drink

People need to drink water every day. Fruit juice is a tasty cold drink. Hot drinks made from milk give you plenty of energy.

Sweet things

Many people enjoy eating sugary food such as cakes, sweets, and biscuits. But eating too much sugar can be bad for you.

This salad is made from fresh lettuce, tomatoes, and cucumber.

Fruit

Fruit is filled with vitamins. Fruit is naturally sweet and makes a healthy snack.

cake

apple

banana

pear

grapes

orange

Growing food

Much of our food comes from crops grown by farmers in different parts of the world. Some farmers grow cereals and plants in open fields. Others grow vegetables and fruit in special buildings called greenhouses.

Sunflower

Sunflowers produce hundreds of seeds. The seeds are squeezed to give us oil for cooking.

Cereal

Cereals are grasses that are grown for their seeds. The seeds are called grain. Grain is used to make flour for bread, pasta, and cakes.

oats   rye   barley   wheat

Growing grain

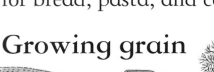

Sowing
Farmers plough their fields with tractors before they sow the grain seeds.

Ripening
The seeds grow into plants. New seeds grow on the plants and ripen in the sun.

Harvesting
The farmers use combine harvesters to separate the ripe grain from the stems.

Sugar cane

Sugar cane is a giant grass that grows in hot countries. The thick stem is called cane and is full of sweet juice. The juice is used to make sugar.

Rice

rice terrace

Rice is grown in fields flooded with water, called paddy fields. These rice farmers have cut big steps, or terraces, into steep hillsides to make flat paddy fields.

Pod vegetables

Vegetables such as peas and beans are seeds that grow inside the seed pod of a plant. They are picked out of the pod and frozen, tinned, dried, or eaten fresh.

tomato

bean

Salad vegetables

In cold countries lettuces, cucumbers, tomatoes, and celery are grown in greenhouses to protect them from bad weather.

Root vegetables

Some plants have tasty roots that we can eat. Potatoes, beetroot, parsnips, and carrots are all root vegetables.

Green vegetables

Cabbages, cauliflowers, and broccoli are grown in fields. They grow well in places that have a lot of rain.

cabbage

banana plant

apple trees

date palm

grape vines

Tropical fruit

Some fruit grows in hot countries. Bananas grow in bunches on tall plants. Dates grow on palm trees.

Orchards

Fruits such as apples, oranges, and pears grow on trees. Farmers grow a lot of fruit trees together in orchards.

Vineyards

Grapes grow on vines in special fields called vineyards. Grapes are eaten fresh, or crushed to make juice or wine.

Going shopping

Very few people can make or grow all the things they need. In the past, people swapped with one another to get the things they needed. Today, people use money to buy what they need. Some shops, such as bakeries, sell only one kind of thing. Others, such as supermarkets, sell many different things.

Bakery
People go to the bakery to buy fresh bread. Some bakers sell pies and cakes, too.

At the supermarket

Choosing
Supermarkets are filled with thousands of things to buy. Shoppers choose what they need from the shelves.

Special counters
Sometimes there are special counters in the supermarket where shoppers can buy fresh fish, meat, and cheese.

Paying
At the check-out counter, the cashier uses a cash register to add up how much the shopper must pay.

Shopping basket
People need to go shopping regularly to buy food and other things for their homes. Before they go to the shops they work out what to buy. Many people make a list of all the things they need.

People use money, a cheque, a debit card, or a credit card to pay for their shopping.

Most food is packed in tins, bags, boxes, or bottles.

Toy shop

A toy shop is packed with all sorts of different toys and games, from teddy bears, puzzles, and toy planes to bats, balls, and skipping ropes. Some children save up all their pocket money to buy toys and games.

Bookshop

Many bookshops have a comfortable corner where you can sit and take time to decide which books you would like to buy.

Shoe shop

In a shoe shop you can choose a new pair of shoes, sandals, or boots in the colour and style you like best. It is important to buy shoes that are the right size.

The shoe-shop assistant checks the size of your feet to make sure that your shoes fit properly.

Florist

A florist sells flowers and plants. If you buy a bunch of flowers as a present, the florist will wrap them in pretty paper.

Department store

Department stores are huge shops that are divided up into different sections. People can buy all sorts of things in a department store – from clothes and hats, to stationery and furniture.

Clothes we wear

We wear clothes to keep us comfortable throughout the day and night. People choose different clothes to wear in hot or cold weather, and special clothes for work or for play.

woolly hat

scarf

gloves

Clothes for night and day

We wear loose-fitting clothes to sleep in at night. In the morning, we get dressed in different clothes. First we put on underwear. Then we put on clothes to suit what we do during the day.

coat

sweatshirt

nightdress

vest

skirt

trousers

slippers

pants

socks

shoes

boots

dressing gown

Uniforms

People wear uniforms to show that they belong to a certain group or do the same job. People such as waiters usually wear a uniform.

waiter

band players

Cold weather clothes

In cold weather we wear extra layers of clothes. Warm air is trapped between the layers and keeps out the cold. When we go outside, we can dress warmly in a thick coat and a woolly hat, scarf, and gloves.

Very cold places

People who live in very cold countries, such as Tibet, wear many thick layers of clothing made from fur, wool, or felt.

Very hot places

In very hot countries, such as Egypt, people often wear long, flowing robes made from white cotton to keep cool. They cover their heads to protect them from the sun.

Hot weather clothes

We need fewer clothes when the weather is hot. We wear loose-fitting clothes, such as a sundress or a sari, so that air can move around our bodies and keep us cool. Hot weather clothes are usually made from light fabrics such as cotton.

Safe, clean, and dry

We wear some clothes for special reasons. A bicycle helmet protects your head if you fall off your bike. An apron keeps your everyday clothes clean when you do messy jobs such as painting or cooking. A raincoat keeps you dry in wet weather.

helmet

apron

raincoat

sundress

A sari is an Indian dress made from a single piece of fabric.

sandals

Festival clothes

Many people wear brightly coloured and decorated clothes to festivals and other special events. This Japanese girl is wearing a robe called a yukata to celebrate a summer festival.

Jobs people do

Most people have to work to earn money to pay for a home, food, and clothes. There are thousands of different jobs to do. People try to find a job that they will do well and enjoy.

Scientist
Scientists try to find out more about the world around us and how it works. This scientist works in a laboratory, looking for cures for diseases.

Librarian
Librarians buy and take care of the books in a library. They make sure that all the books are in the right place so that we can find them easily.

The librarian stamps the books we borrow. The date shows when we must return the books.

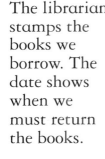

Hairdresser
Hairdressers look after and style people's hair. They are trained to wash, colour, curl, and cut hair.

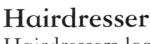

Jobs in a car factory

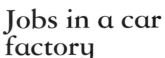
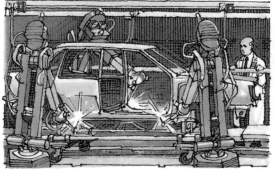

Designer
The designer thinks up ideas for how a car will look and makes detailed drawings of each part.

Machine operator
The machine operator works the machines that cut out the metal parts of the car and weld them together.

Assembly line worker
Assembly line workers work in a team to put together, or assemble, all the different parts of each car.

Firefighter

Firefighters work in a team to put out fires. They drive a fire engine to the scene of the fire and pump water through large hoses to put out the flames.

Chef

A chef is an expert cook who is in charge of making the food served in hotels and restaurants. Chefs wear special hats and coats to keep clean and tidy while they are cooking.

Musician

A musician plays an instrument such as a violin. Some musicians play on their own as a soloist. Others play with lots of other musicians in an orchestra or band.

Plumber

A plumber's job is to put in and repair the water pipes attached to the baths, basins, drains, and lavatories in our homes and workplaces.

Office worker

Some people do their jobs in an office. They work at a desk and may use a computer to help them.

Supervisor

The supervisor makes sure that the assembly line workers are doing their jobs properly.

Quality tester

The quality tester checks the finished car and makes sure that everything is working correctly.

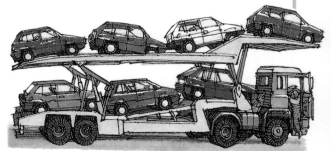

Driver

The driver's job is to drive the car transporter, loaded with new cars, to the place where they will be sold.

Towns and cities

Towns and cities are busy places, where millions of people live and work. Towns are filled with buildings that are used for different things. People work in offices, shops, and factories; live in houses and apartments; and relax and enjoy themselves in cinemas, cafés, theatres, and parks.

Factory

Factories are often built on the outskirts of a town. This means that lorries delivering to the factories do not have to drive through the heavy traffic in the city centre.

Town hall

In most towns, there is a town hall. The people who look after the town work in offices in the town hall. There are also large rooms for meetings and special events.

School

There are schools and colleges for children of all ages in a town. Children go to school to learn. All school buildings look different. This modern school has room for hundreds of pupils.

City centre

There are all sorts of places to visit on either side of a busy street in the city – from cafés, shops, and cinemas, to crowded street markets and quiet parks.

A **cinema** shows films, usually in the afternoons and evenings.

A **market** is a busy place where people buy all sorts of things – from fruit and flowers, to clothes and furniture.

A **café** is a place where people can go to eat and drink, meet their friends, and watch the world go by.

Places of worship

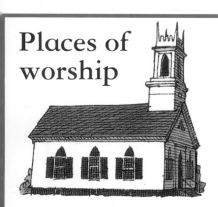

Church
Christians gather to pray and sing in a church. The main services are usually on Sundays.

Temple
One fifth of all the people in the world are Buddhists. They worship in temples and monasteries.

Synagogue
Jewish people worship in synagogues. The main services are usually on Fridays and Saturdays.

Mosque
Muslim people worship in a mosque. They pray five times a day, facing the holy city of Mecca.

Office block
An office block is often built in the middle of a crowded city. Lots of different businesses can have their offices in one building.

scaffolding

wheel loader

cement mixer

Building site
In most cities, there are many building sites where new shops, houses, and offices are being built. Builders use special machinery and trucks to get the buildings ready.

Parks are peaceful gardens where city people can escape from the crowded streets and noisy traffic.

A hospital is a place where sick and injured people go to be cared for. Nurses and doctors look after them and try to make them well again. People often go to hospital in an ambulance.

In the countryside

Out in the country there are open fields, hills, and forests full of trees, plants, insects, birds, and other wildlife. There are fewer roads and houses than in the city, and the air is fresh and clean.

Bat

Bats are furry animals with wings. They sleep during the day, hanging upside down. At night, they hunt and eat insects and other small animals.

Dragonfly

A dragonfly flies faster than any other insect. It swoops and hovers over ponds and streams, catching and eating other insects.

Camping

In warm weather it is fun to camp out-of-doors in a tent. People pitch their tents in special places called campsites.

Frog

A frog is an amphibian. This means that it can live in water and on land. Frogs eat worms and insects, which they catch with their long, sticky tongues.

Most campers sleep in zip-up eiderdowns called sleeping bags.

A pond is a pool of still water. It is home to many small fish, insects, birds, and other creatures.

Living in the countryside

In the countryside people live in small towns or villages, or on farms. It is usually peaceful and quiet in the country.

Hiking

Hikers enjoy walking long distances in the countryside. They wear strong walking boots and thick socks. Hikers carry the food they need for the day in bags called rucksacks.

Owl

The tawny owl hunts at night. It uses its powerful feet and claws, called talons, to catch mice and birds to eat.

Birdwatcher

Birdwatchers sit quietly, watching wild birds eat, make nests, feed their chicks, and fly from branch to branch. Birdwatchers can use binoculars to help them to see the birds more clearly.

Fox

A fox has good eyesight, which helps it to hunt at night. It catches rabbits and birds to eat.

Rabbit

Wild rabbits live together under the ground in a network of passages and holes called a warren. They come out at night to eat grass and other plants.

Canoeing

Canoeists paddle along rivers in long, narrow boats called canoes. They can take time to look at the plants and wildlife around them.

Plants

There are millions of plants in the world. We use them for food, to make clothes, and as medicine. A plant is made up of a stem with leaves and flowers, and roots that grow under the ground.

Flowers are the part of a plant that makes seeds.

Leaves grow from the plant's stem.

Growing flowers

Planting
Flower seeds are planted in holes in the ground. Then the seeds are covered with soil and watered well.

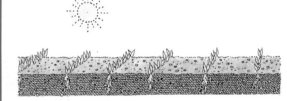

Sprouting
As the ground is warmed by the sun, the seeds begin to sprout. Shoots appear above the ground and roots grow into the soil.

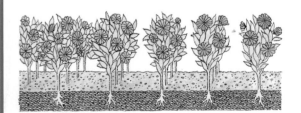

Flowering
Leaves begin to grow from the shoots. As the plant grows taller, buds appear. The buds swell and open into flowers.

Flowers
Most plants have flowers on their stems. People grow flowering plants, such as roses, because they look and smell lovely. Some flowers, such as the blossom on apple trees, turn into fruit that we can eat.

rose

apple blossom

Seeds and bulbs
When a flower dies, it leaves behind a seed head filled with tiny seeds. The seeds drop to the ground and grow into new plants. Some plants, such as daffodils, grow from bulbs instead of seeds. Some bulbs grow a new part every year, which forms a new plant.

seed head

seeds

pod

stem

bulb

Roots take water from the soil.

Pot plants

Some people decorate their homes with plants grown in pots. Pot plants grow best in a room with plenty of sunlight. People need to take special care to keep their pot plants healthy.

People often choose pot plants with colourful or patterned leaves to grow in their homes.

parsley

mint

lavender

Herbs

Herbs are useful plants. They can be used to make natural medicines or chopped up and cooked to flavour food. Some herbs are crushed and their oils are used to make perfume.

Creepers are plants that can climb up walls.

Window box

Many people grow flowers and plants in narrow boxes. They put the boxes on a window sill in the sun. The plants grow well in the warmth and light, but they need plenty of water.

Wild flowers

Wild flowers grow by themselves. Their seeds are carried by the wind or by animals. When the seeds reach the ground, they grow into new plants.

Garden

Some people have their own gardens where they can grow their favourite plants and flowers. They dig flower beds and spend time watering, weeding, and taking care of their plants.

37

Minibeasts

The tiny creatures that live in our gardens, in parks, and in the countryside, are sometimes called minibeasts. There are thousands of different minibeasts – from flying insects, such as bees and flies, to climbing spiders and snails that crawl along the ground.

Most spiders spin a sticky web between the branches of trees or bushes. Spiders lie in wait to catch insects that fly into their webs.

Spider

All spiders have eight legs. They catch and eat small flying insects, such as gnats, flies, and moths.

A spider kills its prey with a poisonous bite.

Fly

Like most insects, flies have six legs. They have only one pair of wings. Flies can flap their wings so fast that they seem to stay still in the air.

Snail

A snail glides along the ground on one large foot, leaving a trail of slime behind it. In times of danger, it can hide its soft body inside the hard shell on its back.

A snail's eyes are on the end of its feelers.

Ladybird

A ladybird is a small beetle. It has dark spots on its brightly coloured wing cases. Ladybirds eat smaller insects.

On the ground

Beneath our feet live hundreds of minibeasts. Ants and beetles scurry along looking for food, slugs glide slowly through the grass, and worms burrow into the earth.

Earthworms help to keep the soil healthy by making holes that let air and water into the ground.

Butterfly life-cycle

Caterpillar
A female butterfly lays eggs on a plant. The eggs hatch out into caterpillars, which eat the plant's leaves.

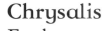

Chrysalis
Each caterpillar grows big and fat. Its skin hardens and it turns into a chrysalis or pupa.

Butterfly
After a few weeks, the pupa splits. A butterfly climbs out. When its wings dry, it flies away.

Grasshopper
Grasshoppers are insects. They can jump long distances, using their powerful back legs. The grasshopper's green colour helps it to hide in long grass.

Bee
Honeybees live in a large group called a colony. Each colony has one queen bee who lays the eggs. Worker bees collect sweet juices from flowers to make honey.

When bees fly, the flapping of their wings makes a buzzing sound.

Bees make wax honeycombs for storing their honey.

Hiding
Some insects match their surroundings, which helps them to hide from their enemies. A leaf butterfly is hard to spot in a leafy tree or bush. A stick insect looks exactly like a plant stem.

leaf butterfly

stick insect

Trees

A tree is a tall plant with a woody stem called a trunk. Trees are the largest living things in the world and can live for hundreds of years. A group of many trees growing together is called a forest.

Tree

Trees with leaves that turn brown and drop off in the autumn are called deciduous trees. Trees with narrow leaves that stay green on the tree all year round are called conifers or evergreens.

deciduous tree   conifer

Leaf

There are two kinds of leaf. Thin, waxy leaves called needles grow on conifers. Broad leaves grow on deciduous trees. These can be simple leaves, or compound leaves made up of lots of leaflets growing from one stem.

compound leaf

simple leaf

trunk

pine needles

Tree trunk

Every year, a tree trunk grows another layer of wood, which makes a ring. People can count the rings to find out how many years the tree has been alive.

This is a sideways slice of a tree's trunk, showing its rings.

chestnut

peach

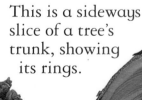

acorn

Tree fruit

All trees grow fruit of some kind. The fruit drops from the tree and is scattered by the wind or carried away by animals. Inside the fruit are seeds or pips. If they reach the soil they can grow into new, young trees.

pine cone

wasp's nest

branch

Timber

Some trees are grown especially for their wood, or timber. When the trees are big enough, they are chopped down. The trunks, or logs, are taken to a saw mill where they are cut into flat strips, called planks.

A logging truck takes the logs to the saw mill.

Tree house

A tree is home to all sorts of creatures. Birds roost and nest in the branches. Squirrels run up and down the tree trunk and make leafy nests called dreys. Insects buzz around in the treetops or scuttle about among the roots.

Bark is the tree's skin. It protects the tree from insects and diseases.

Wild rabbits live in a warren, which is a network of underground holes, or burrows. The entrance to a rabbit warren is often hidden in the roots of a tall tree.

chair

plank

Things made from wood

Many useful things are made from wood. Wooden planks are used for building, or making furniture such as chairs. Wood chips are crushed into pulp to make paper. Fewer trees need to be cut down if old paper is saved and used to make new paper.

woodchips

book

Natural forest

For thousands of years, trees have grown naturally in forests all over the world. Trees are very important because they give off oxygen that all animals, including humans, need to breathe.

Birds

Birds are the only animals that have feathers. All birds have wings, but not all of them can fly. Some birds live together in large groups called flocks, while others live alone.

Breeding

Laying

Female birds lay eggs, often in a nest built high in a tree. The female or male bird sits on the eggs to keep them warm.

Hatching

When a baby bird, or chick, hatches from the egg, its eyes are usually closed. Many chicks have no feathers.

Growing

The male and female birds fly back and forth with food for the chicks. When the chicks' feathers grow, they can fly and feed themselves.

Flight

Most birds have perfect bodies for flying. Their hollow bones are light and very strong. Birds fly by flapping their wings or by gliding on currents of air. Some birds can flap their wings so fast that they hover in the air.

Feather

A bird has different kinds of feather. Tail and wing feathers help the bird to fly. The outer feathers are special colours to hide the bird from its enemies or help the bird to show off to its mate. Soft down feathers grow close to the bird's body to keep it warm.

tail feather

body feather

down feather

Kiwi

A kiwi's wings are so small that it cannot fly. It lives and nests on the ground. A kiwi hunts at night. It uses the nostrils at the end of its beak to sniff out food in the dark.

Feeding
Many wild birds feed on berries, insects, and seeds. Some people feed the birds by putting seeds, bread, and nuts in their gardens.

Falcon
A falcon is a bird of prey, which means that it eats meat. Its sharp beak and claws help it to catch and eat small animals.

Parakeet
Brightly coloured parakeets live in tropical rainforests. They use their strong, hooked beaks to crack open the seeds and nuts that they eat.

Pelican
Pelicans live on river banks and on the seashore. A pelican's beak has a stretchy pouch, which it uses like a fishing net to scoop up fish to eat.

Flamingo
Flamingos live together in big flocks beside lakes and marshes. They wade through the water on their long legs.

Duck
Ducks live near ponds and rivers. The toes of their feet are joined with flaps of skin. They use these webbed feet as paddles to swim along.

A duck dips its beak into the water to find insects, worms, and plants to eat.

Farm animals

Many kinds of animal are kept on farms. We get milk, eggs, and wool from the animals. Some are killed for their meat. It is the farmers' job to feed and care for the animals so that they stay healthy.

Sheep

Sheep live together in groups called flocks. They graze on grass in fields or paddocks. A ewe is a female sheep and a ram is a male sheep.

Sheepdog

The sheepdog's job is to help the farmer round up the sheep in the fields. The farmer calls and whistles to the dog to tell it what to do.

A lamb is a baby sheep.

Wool farming

Growing a fleece

During the cold winter months, sheep grow a thick woolly coat called a fleece.

Rounding up

In the spring, farmers and their dogs round up the sheep, ready to be sheared.

Shearing

Farmers shear the sheep, cutting off their fleece. The fleece is spun into wool.

Goat

Goats are good climbers and can live on steep hillsides. Farmers keep goats for their milk, which is turned into cheese.

A nanny goat is a female goat.

A kid is a baby goat.

Piglets are baby pigs.

Pig

Pigs are kept for their meat, which is called pork. Pigs live in sties and eat vegetables and cereal. A female pig is called a sow. She can have more than 15 piglets at a time!

A cockerel is a male chicken.

Chicken

Female chickens are called hens. A hen lays an egg nearly every day. Farmers collect the eggs and sell them to shops where we can buy the eggs.

A chick is a baby chicken.

Cattle

Cattle are kept for their meat, which is called beef. Cattle live in large groups called herds. They graze on open grasslands on big farms called ranches or stations.

Bulls and oxen are male cattle.

Cow

Female cattle are called cows. Farmers keep cows for their milk. Cows live in herds and graze in fields. They need to be milked every day.

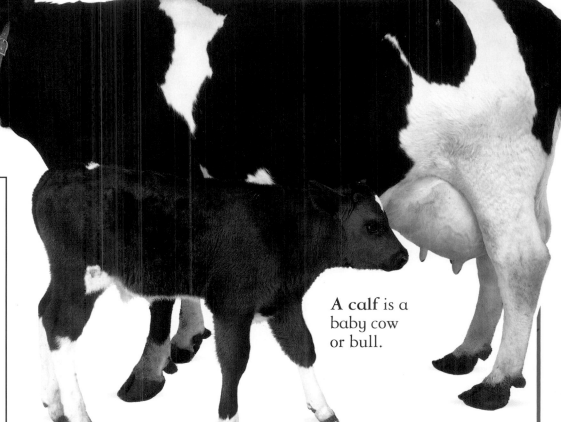

A calf is a baby cow or bull.

Dairy food

One cow can give us 14 litres of milk every day. Dairy foods, such as butter, yoghurt, and cheese, are made from milk.

milk   butter   yoghurt   cheese

45

At the seaside

The seaside is the place where the land meets the sea. Colourful shells and seaweed are washed up on to the beaches, and curious sea creatures, such as starfish and sea anemones, live in rocky pools.

winkle   tower shell   top shell

Shell

Many kinds of shell can be found on the beach. Shells are the homes of sea creatures. Some people collect empty shells with bright colours or interesting shapes.

cone shell   scallop   whelk

Starfish

Starfish have five arms. The suckers under their arms help the starfish to cling to rocks under the water.

Starfish also use their arms to pull apart shellfish to eat.

Changing tides

Twice a day, at high tide, the sea level rises. At low tide the sea runs back down the beach, leaving a line of seaweed and shells behind.

Fun on the beach

A sandy beach is the best kind for playing and sunbathing. You can build sandcastles on the soft sand and paddle in the shallow water.

Seaweed

Seaweed is a sea plant. Green seaweed grows in shallow water. Brown seaweed usually grows in deeper water.

Moving house

A hermit crab does not have a shell to protect its soft body.

It has to find the shell of a dead sea animal to live in.

When it finds a shell that fits, the crab climbs in.

Crab

Crabs have ten legs. They use eight legs to swim and scuttle sideways across the sand. A crab's two front legs end in sharp claws called pincers.

A crab uses its pincers to catch and eat small sea animals.

A crab has a hard shell to protect its soft body.

Seagull

Seagulls keep their eggs safe by nesting in groups high up in the cliffs. Seagulls swoop down and dive into the sea for food.

Cliff

Steep, rocky cliffs are found on coasts where crashing waves have worn away the land.

Rock pool

When the tide goes out on a rocky coast, pools of seawater are trapped in the rocks. These rock pools are home to many kinds of sea creature.

sea anemone

rockpool fish

mussel

rock pool

In the sea

The world under the sea is filled with strange and beautiful creatures and plants. Some sea animals, such as dolphins, swim near the surface of the water while others, such as shrimps, crawl along the sea bed.

Dolphin

Dolphins are not fish – they are mammals. They live underwater, but swim to the surface to breathe. Dolphins can leap right out of the water.

Sharks use their sense of smell to find food.

Shark

Most sharks have large jaws, lined with rows of very sharp teeth. They eat fish and other sea animals.

Sea horse

A sea horse is a tiny fish. It swims upright, using its small fins as paddles. A sea horse grips seaweed with its tail to stay very still and watch out for food. It sucks up food into its tube-shaped mouth.

Octopus

An octopus has eight long tentacles covered with suckers. These help the octopus to move over rocks and hold its prey. An octopus also uses its tentacles to feel and taste.

Shrimp

A shrimp has a hard shell that covers and protects its soft body. This shrimp lives on the sea bed. It digs a hole in the sand to hide from its enemies.

Plankton

Plankton is the name for tiny sea animals and plants. They are so small that they cannot be seen without a magnifying glass. Plankton is an important food for many sea creatures.

animal plankton

plant plankton

These pictures show plankton much bigger than it really is.

Fishing boat

Fishing boats use huge nets to catch thousands of fish at a time. The people who work on the boats must take care not to catch too many fish, because one day there could be no fish left.

net

Diver

Scuba divers are people who like to explore under the sea. They wear tight, waterproof suits to keep them warm. Divers carry air tanks and wear masks so that they can breathe and see underwater.

tentacles

Jellyfish

A jellyfish uses its long tentacles to sting plankton or small fish. It carries its prey to its mouth in the centre of its soft body.

Tropical fish

This fish lives in the warm, shallow waters of a tropical coral reef. It swims in large groups called shoals.

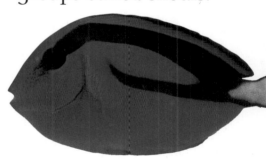

Shipwrecks are fascinating places for divers to explore. Divers hunt for objects that sank with the ship and try to work out what the ship looked like before it was wrecked.

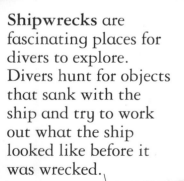

Coral reef

A coral reef takes thousands of years to form. It is built up from the skeletons of millions of tiny animals called coral polyps. A coral reef is home to all sorts of different sea creatures.

Seasons and weather

There are four seasons every year – spring, summer, autumn, and winter. Each season brings changes in the weather. As the weather changes, the plants and animals begin to change, too.

A rainbow appears when sunlight shines through a rain shower.

Spring

In spring, the world comes to life after the cold winter. The days grow longer and the weather gets warmer. Blossom appears on some trees and many birds return from their winter homes in other lands.

People should never look straight at the Sun. Its light is so bright that it can damage the eyes.

Many people use umbrellas and wear boots to keep dry in the rain.

Sun

Sun

The hot Sun gives out light and heat. Its energy helps to make the trees and plants grow. But the Sun can be harmful, too. People need to protect their skin from its strong rays by using a sun protection cream.

Rain

The clouds in the sky are full of tiny drops of water. When the drops get too big and heavy, they fall to the ground as rain. There are often showers of rain in the spring.

Summer

Summer is the hottest season. There are leaves on the trees and the flowers bloom. Many people spend time out-of-doors, enjoying the long, sunny days.

Storm

During a storm, dark clouds gather. There are loud bangs called thunder. Flashes of lightning light up the sky.

Strong winds often blow during a storm.

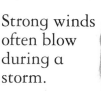

Wind

Wind is moving air. Wind can be a light breeze, or a strong gale. It is fun to fly a kite on a windy day.

In the autumn many birds fly away to warmer lands.

Autumn

In autumn, the wind gets colder and the days become shorter. Leaves fall off the trees. Some animals grow thicker fur to get ready for the cold winter.

Leaves

The leaves on some trees change colour in different seasons. In spring, the leaves are pale green. In summer, they turn bright green, and in autumn, they turn orange, then brown, then they fall off the tree.

Snow

When the air is very cold, the drops of water in the clouds freeze. They turn into icy crystals that join up and fall to the ground as snowflakes. Snowflakes pile up into a layer of snow that covers the ground.

Winter

Winter is the coldest season of the year. Most trees are bare and many plants stop growing. People need to heat their homes and wear thicker clothes to keep warm. The freezing winds often bring snow and ice.

The world we live in

The world is made up of land and sea. The land is divided into seven big areas called continents. The Equator is an imaginary line around the middle of the world. Most of the land near the Equator is hot all year round. Far away from the Equator, the lands near the North and South Poles are icy cold.

Globe and map

A globe is a model of the world, showing all the different continents and oceans. A map is a flat picture of the round world, showing the same things.

North Pole

South Pole

Equator

Desert

Deserts are the hottest and driest places in the world. They cover about one fifth of all the land. Deserts are boiling hot during the day and bitterly cold at night.

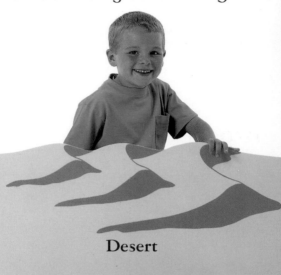

Desert

Map of the world

This map shows the continents and oceans of the Earth.

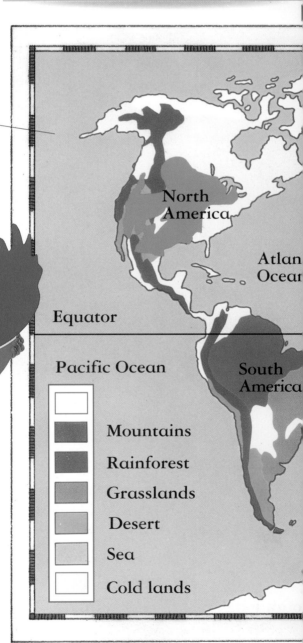

North America

Atlantic Ocean

Equator

Pacific Ocean

South America

Mountains
Rainforest
Grasslands
Desert
Sea
Cold lands

Sea

Sea

Three quarters of the world's surface is covered by salt water called the sea. The sea is made up of different oceans. The Pacific Ocean is the largest and the deepest ocean. The oceans all join up, so it is possible to sail right round the world without touching land.

Grasslands

Grasslands are flat, dry plains often found between deserts and forests. The largest area of grassland stretches from Europe to Asia.

Grasslands

Mountains

Tall, rocky mountains often form part of a mountain range, either on land or under the sea. The tallest mountain in the world is Mount Everest in Asia.

Mountains

Rainforest

Rainforests grow in hot, wet parts of the world. Nearly half of all the different plants and animals in the world live in rainforest jungles.

Rainforest

Cold lands

The North and South Poles are the coldest places in the world. At the South Pole, there is a continent called Antarctica, but at the North Pole, there is just an enormous piece of ice floating in the sea.

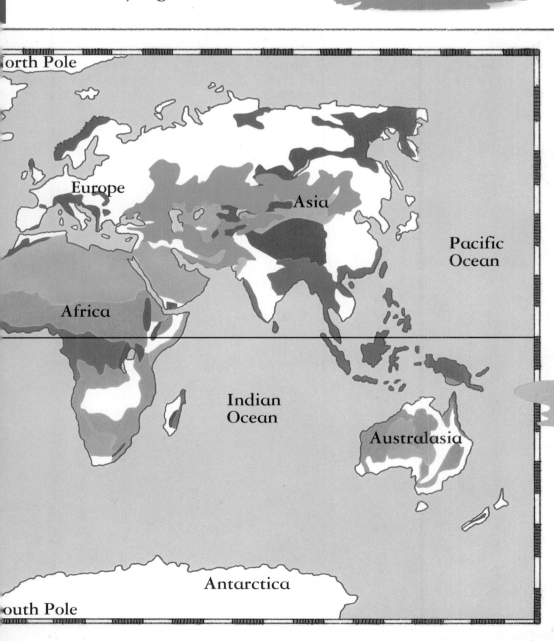

North Pole

Europe

Asia

Pacific Ocean

Africa

Indian Ocean

Australasia

Antarctica

South Pole

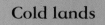

Cold lands

Children of the world

There are millions of children in the world. About 150 babies are born every minute! The children on these pages live in cities on different continents and speak different languages, but their days are filled with school, sports, and play, just like many other children all over the world.

Trafalgar Square in London, the capital of the United Kingdom.

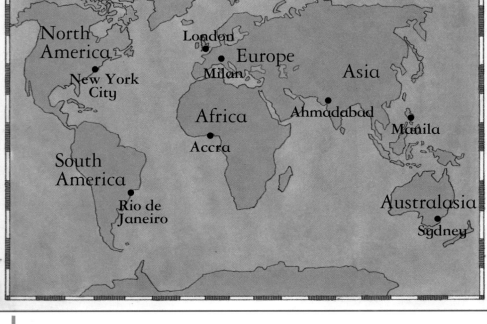

Robert and Anna from Europe

Robert lives in London in the United Kingdom. He speaks English. His friend, Anna, comes from Milan in Italy and she speaks Italian. They are spending the day together, visiting all the sights of London.

John and Emma from North America

John and Emma live in New York City, the biggest city in the United States of America. John and Emma speak English. Today is Saturday. John and Emma are going to watch a basketball game.

Skyscrapers in New York City in the United States.

Adriana from South America

Adriana lives in Rio de Janeiro in Brazil. She speaks Portuguese. Adriana loves to play tennis after school. She wants to be a tennis champion when she is older.

Sugar Loaf Mountain in Rio de Janeiro, Brazil.

Hiral from South Asia

Hiral lives in Ahmadabad in the Gujarat region of India. He speaks Gujarati. Hiral and his friends enjoy playing cricket after school. They practise hard every day.

Rani Sipri's Mosque in Ahmadabad in India.

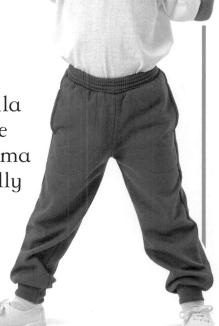

Rizal Park in Manila, the capital of the Philippines.

Gemma from South-East Asia

Gemma lives in Manila in the Philippines. She speaks Tagalog. Gemma enjoys school, especially gym class. Today she is trying out some new exercises.

Independence Arch in Accra, the capital of Ghana.

The Opera House and the Harbour Bridge in Sydney, Australia.

Adjoa from Africa

Adjoa lives in Accra in Ghana. She speaks Twi. Today is Adjoa's first day at school. She is looking forward to learning interesting things and making new friends.

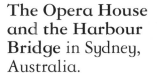

Dan and Laura from Australasia.

Dan and Laura live in Sydney in Australia. They both speak English. It's a lovely sunny day. They are off for a boat ride in the harbour.

In the desert

A desert is a place where almost no rain falls. Only animals and plants that need very little water can live in a desert.

Oil wells are drilled in some deserts to pump oil from deep under the ground.

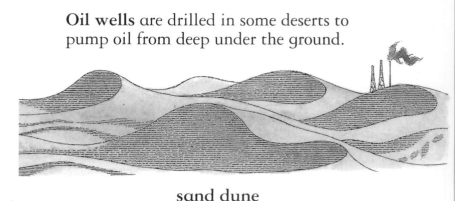

sand dune

Sandy desert

Sandy deserts are covered in hills of shifting sand called dunes. Very few plants grow in these hot, dry lands.

palm tree

water well

An oasis is a place in the desert where water is found. People build a town around an oasis.

Beetle

This beetle has yellow wing cases that make it hard to see on the desert sand. Its long legs hold its body off the hot sand.

Camel

A camel can survive for days without food or water. It lives on the fat stored in its hump. This camel is called a dromedary and has one hump. It lives in the deserts of Africa, the Middle East, and Australia.

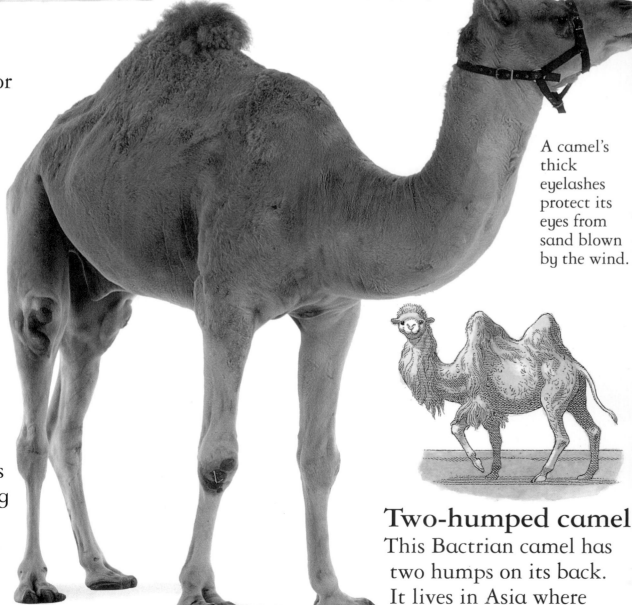

A camel's thick eyelashes protect its eyes from sand blown by the wind.

Scorpion

A scorpion has a poisonous sting in its tail. It hunts at night, searching for insects to eat.

Two-humped camel

This Bactrian camel has two humps on its back. It lives in Asia where the desert is cooler.

Tuareg people

The Tuareg people of Africa live in goatskin tents in the Sahara desert. They are nomads, moving from place to place to find grass for their camels and goats. Tuareg people use camels to carry their belongings across the desert.

Tuareg people hang their belongings in trees to keep them safe from animals.

Rocky desert

In some deserts the land is rocky and bare. Only plants that store their own water, such as cacti, grow in the dry, rocky deserts of North America.

This rattlesnake buries itself in the sand to keep cool during the very hot days.

Rattlesnake

A rattlesnake gets its name from the rattle on the end of its tail. It shakes its tail from side to side to warn other animals to keep away.

Cactus

A Saguaro cactus grows very slowly. It can live for up to two hundred years and grow taller than a house.

Elf owls nest in holes in the tall cactus plant.

Lizard

This desert lizard has sharp spines on its back. These spines protect it from attack.

Strong, dry winds blow across the desert plains and carve the rocks into strange shapes.

Rat

During the day, the kangaroo rat stays in its burrow to keep cool.

In the grasslands

Grasslands are flat plains where grass, low bushes, and few trees grow. The summers are very hot and dry, while the winters are cold. The grasslands are home to many different animals, from plant-eating elephants and zebras, to meat-eating animals such as lions.

Zebra

Zebras live in large groups called herds. While the rest of the herd grazes, the leaders watch out for danger.

Elephant

An African elephant is the biggest animal that lives on land. The elephant's nose and upper lip form a long, supple trunk. It uses its trunk like a hand to pick plants and put them into its mouth.

An elephant also uses its trunk to squirt water into its mouth.

African savannah

The driest areas of grassland are called savannah. The African savannah is one of the last places left in the world where there are still large herds of wild animals. Hundreds of animals gather at water holes to drink.

A giraffe's long legs and neck help it to reach the leaves at the tops of tall trees.

A hippopotamus keeps cool by lying in a water hole with just its eyes, nose, and ears showing above the surface.

kob

topi

wildebeest

Vulture

A vulture is a bird of prey with very good eyesight. It flies high above the grasslands, searching for dead animals to eat.

Lion

Lions lie in wait at a water hole to pounce on animals that come to drink. They spend the rest of their time asleep in the shade.

Children look after the cattle. They move them around to find fresh grass.

Xhosa people

Many Xhosa people live in villages on the grasslands of southern Africa. They use mud and branches from the plains to build their houses. Living in these barren lands can be difficult. The men often have to leave the family to try to find work in the cities.

Many Xhosa women stay in the villages to look after the crops.

Australian grasslands

Animals such as kangaroos, wallabies, and dingoes live on the hot, dry plains of central Australia. Tall eucalyptus trees grow on the banks of rivers, or creeks, and are home to flocks of brightly coloured birds.

galah

Dingoes are a type of wild dog. They hunt together in groups called packs.

Emus are the second largest birds in the world. They cannot fly, but they run very fast on flat ground.

Kangaroo

A kangaroo uses its long tail to balance as it leaps over the ground. A baby kangaroo, or joey, is carried in a special pouch on its mother's stomach.

In the rainforest

Rainforests grow in hot and rainy parts of the world. Millions of animals live among the thick undergrowth and tall trees. Some live high up in the treetops, where they can see the sun. Here, the leaves and plants make a kind of roof called a canopy.

Tree frog

This tiny frog lives in the forest canopy. It grips the leaves with its sticky fingers and toes.

Canopy plant

This plant grows at the top of tall trees. It lives off rainwater, which collects in its curved leaves.

Hummingbird

A hummingbird beats its wings so fast that they make a humming sound. Hummingbirds hover in the air and sip sweet juice, called nectar, from flowers.

A hummingbird uses its long beak to reach deep inside flowers.

Jaguar

A jaguar is a big wild cat. It can climb trees and swim. The jaguar's spotted coat makes it difficult to see as it stalks through the shady rainforest.

Ants

These ants march along the forest floor. They bite off pieces of leaf to carry back to their nest.

Snake

This snake is called a python. It eats small animals and birds. The python climbs trees by coiling itself around branches.

Monkey

There are many kinds of monkey living in the rainforest. This monkey uses its arms and tail to swing from branch to branch.

Sloth

A sloth moves very slowly. It spends most of its life hanging upside down in trees. The sloth grips the branches with its long, hooked claws.

Butterfly

This butterfly lives in the canopy of the rainforest. Its colourful wings make it easy to spot as it flies through shafts of sunlight.

Yanomami people

Some Yanomami people still follow a traditional way of life in remote parts of the rainforest in South America. They hunt animals and birds, gather food such as berries and fruit from the forest, and plant crops in small clearings.

A Yanomami man shows a young child how to plant seeds, using a special digging tool.

This baby caiman has large jaws with more than 100 teeth.

Crocodile

Crocodiles, such as this caiman, live near rivers and swamps. They lie in the shallow water, waiting to catch birds and other animals.

In the mountains

Mountain tops are bare and rocky, and usually covered in snow. The air here is icy cold, so hardly any plants can grow. Animals that can fly or climb, such as eagles and goats, live high up in the mountains. On the lower slopes there are often thick forests, which are home to animals such as bears and wild cats.

Eagles make their nests high up on the mountainside where their eggs will be safe.

Mountaineers wear helmets to protect their heads from falling stones.

Eagle
An eagle is a powerful bird that hunts small animals to eat. Its strong claws, called talons, help it to catch and carry off rabbits, marmots, and squirrels.

Chamois
A chamois is a mountain goat. It has soft pads on its hooves to help it to grip as it climbs up steep, rocky mountains.

A waterfall can be formed when the snow at the top of a mountain melts and the stream of water drops down a steep rock face.

Mountaineer
Some people climb mountains for sport. They use ropes and picks to help them to climb the steep rocks.

Mountain flowers bloom on tiny plants that grow close to the ground. This helps them to shelter from the strong winds.

marmot

Wild cat

Wild cats live in the thick forest on some mountain slopes. They prowl at night, hunting small animals to eat. A wild cat's thick fur keeps it warm in the cold mountain air.

Alpine farmers

In mountains called the Alps, in Europe, some people still farm in the same way as they have done for hundreds of years. In the spring, they move their cattle up into the mountains to graze. In winter, the animals are brought back to shelter in the valleys.

Skier

Skiing is a popular sport in the mountains. A skier wears a pair of long, narrow skis to glide over the snowy slopes.

Ski poles have rings on the ends to keep them from sinking into the soft snow.

Skiers wear padded ski suits and thick boots to help them stay dry and warm.

Bear

The huge brown grizzly bear lives in the mountains of Europe, North America, and Asia. It eats almost anything – from plants, fruit, and berries, to honey, fish, and meat.

Ski lifts or cable cars carry skiers high up the mountainside so that they can ski down the smooth ski slopes.

A brown bear's massive legs end in sharp, hooked claws.

In cold lands

The cold lands near the North and South Poles are covered in ice and snow for most of the year. Few animals and even fewer plants can live in these areas. Animals such as polar bears and huskies have thick fur to keep them warm.

Iceberg

An iceberg is a huge piece of ice that floats in the sea. Most of the iceberg lies below the surface of the water.

Polar bear

Polar bears hunt for food on the Arctic snowfields near the North Pole. They catch seals and fish through holes in the ice. Polar bears use their large, sharp claws to catch and kill their prey.

Polar bears have hair on the soles of their feet to help them to grip the ice.

Inuit people

Inuit people live in the Arctic regions of North America, Greenland, and Russia. Some Inuit people still live by hunting and fishing as they have done for thousands of years.

Summer days in the Arctic are very long. It is dark for only a few hours.

Seal

This seal lives in the Arctic. It swims fast, using its flippers. A thick layer of fat under the seal's skin helps to keep it warm in the icy water.

Husky

A husky is a large dog with a thick, shaggy coat. People who travel near the North Pole use teams of huskies to pull their sledges across the snow.

husky team

Life in Antarctica

The only people who live near the South Pole in Antarctica are explorers or scientists. They study the whales, birds, fish, and other animals that live in the area.

Research stations in the Antarctic have powerful radios. The people who work there use the radios to keep in contact with the rest of the world.

Penguin

Penguins live in Antarctica. They cannot fly, but are fast underwater swimmers. They use their short wings as flippers to speed through the water. Penguins spend most of their lives in the sea, but nest and feed their chicks on land.

Icebreaker ships plough through the frozen seas to open a path for other boats.

Killer whales swim together in groups called pods. They hunt seals, penguins, and squid to eat.

Whale

Many kinds of whale live in the seas around the North and South Poles. A whale swims under water, but comes up to the surface to breathe. It blows stale air out of the blowhole on the top of its head.

Travelling on land

Most people travel on land along roads. Cars, trucks, coaches, and motorbikes speed along, carrying passengers and goods from one place to another. People who need to travel long distances often use wide roads called motorways.

Traffic

Heavy traffic gives off fumes that make the air dirty. This pollution makes it difficult for plants to grow and for people and other animals to breathe.

Truck

Trucks are big vehicles with powerful engines. They can carry heavy loads over long distances. Some trucks have tanks for carrying liquids, others have fridges on board to keep the food they carry fresh.

oil tanker

Car

Many people today travel about in a car. Most cars have four wheels and an engine that runs on petrol or diesel fuel.

This car is called a hatchback. It has a big space behind the back seat for carrying luggage or shopping bags.

Tram

A tram runs on rails down the middle of a street. It carries lots of passengers and can climb up steep hills. Many trams are powered by overhead electric cables.

Animal

Many people travel in carts or carriages pulled by horses, oxen, or donkeys. Some people ride horses to get from place to place.

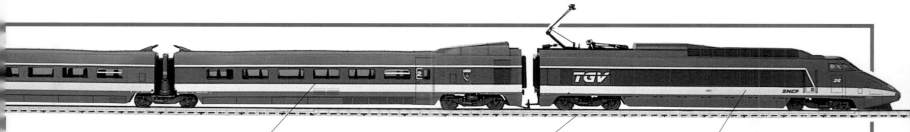

carriage   rails   engine

Train

Travelling by train is quick and safe. The passengers sit in carriages, which are pulled or pushed along the rails by an engine. Trains that travel very long distances have beds in them. They are called sleepers.

Coach

A coach or bus carries lots of people at a time. A coach is used for travelling from town to town, while a bus travels shorter distances within a town.

Camper van

A camper van is like a small mobile house. Inside, there are seats that turn into beds, a cooker, and sometimes even a shower and a lavatory! Many people go on holiday in camper vans.

Bicycle

A bicycle has two wheels that the rider turns by pushing on the pedals. Racing bicycles are light with narrow tyres so that they can go fast. A mountain bike has wider tyres and can be ridden over rough paths and tracks.

Motorbike

A motorbike has two wheels like a bicycle, but it is powered by an engine. Motorbikes can move quickly through heavy traffic and are often used to deliver important packages.

Jeep

A jeep is specially built for driving over soft sand or rough ground. It has a powerful engine and wide, ridged tyres that grip the ground.

Yacht

A yacht is a boat that people sail for fun or in races as a sport. Most yachts have sails. The wind blowing on the sails moves the boat along. Racing yachts are strong and light so that they can speed through the water.

This small yacht can be sailed by one or two people. Large ocean-going yachts usually need many crew members.

Travelling on water

People have invented hundreds of different ways of travelling on water. Big ships and boats carry people and heavy loads long distances far out to sea, while smaller boats, such as yachts, can be sailed on lakes and rivers.

Big propellers push the hovercraft forwards.

Hovercraft

A hovercraft can move over both land and sea on a huge cushion of air. A hovercraft carries passengers on short sea journeys.

Harbour

A harbour is built in a sheltered place on the coast. Ships and boats can safely drop anchor and load and unload their goods and passengers. Tug boats help large ships to steer in and out of the harbour.

A lighthouse warns ships that they are close to shore.

Huge container ships and oil tankers offload their cargo into waiting trucks.

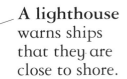

Sailing ship

Before engines were invented, all boats needed sails or oars to move along. Sailing ships are still used to carry goods and passengers along rivers and canals.

This sailing ship is called a dhow. It is used to carry loads along the River Nile in Egypt.

Paddle steamer

Paddle steamers were first built over 100 years ago. A steam engine turns a big wheel that moves the boat forwards.

Speedboat

A speedboat is a small boat with a powerful engine. Its sleek, pointed shape helps it to speed over the water. Speedboats are often used for racing and for sports such as water-skiing.

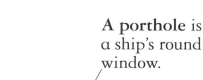

A **porthole** is a ship's round window.

On each deck of the ship there are small boats called lifeboats. These are used to rescue passengers if the ship sinks.

PACIFIC PRINCESS

Cruise liner

Large ships, called liners, carry hundreds of passengers on long holiday cruises. Liners are like floating hotels, with shops, bars, swimming pools, and hundreds of rooms, or cabins, for people to sleep in.

Submarine

Submarines are boats that can travel under the sea. They are often used for exploring under the water. Some submarines can stay underwater for months at a time.

Travelling by air

For hundreds of years people tried to fly. At first, they copied the birds by tying wings to their arms, but they always crashed. About 100 years ago, the first aeroplane took off into the sky. Now, thousands of people travel long distances in aeroplanes every day.

Glider

This plane is a glider. It has no engine. Another plane tows it up into the sky with a cable. When the cable is released, the glider soars through the air.

An aeroplane flight

 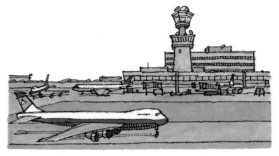

Boarding
Passengers get on board an aeroplane at an airport. Fuel and food for the journey are loaded on to the plane.

Taxiing
The pilot steers the plane down the runway. The control tower tells the pilot when to take off.

Taking off
The plane speeds down the runway until it lifts off the ground. The plane flies to another airport to land.

Helicopter

A helicopter has four blades instead of wings. It can fly straight upwards and hover in the air. This means that a helicopter can take off and land almost anywhere.

The blades whirl round, lifting the helicopter into the air.

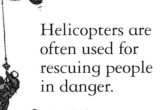

Helicopters are often used for rescuing people in danger.

Seaplane

A seaplane can land on water. It has two floats instead of wheels. Seaplanes are used in places where there is no room for a runway on the land.

Light aircraft

A light aircraft is a small plane. It carries only a few people and can land on short runways. In large countries some people use light aircraft instead of cars to travel long distances.

Concorde

Concorde is a supersonic jet, which means that it can fly faster than the speed of sound. Concorde flies higher and faster than any other passenger plane in the world.

Flight attendant

Flight attendants help to make the plane journey more comfortable for the passengers.

Flight attendants serve food and drinks on long flights.

Flight crew

The pilot and co-pilot are called the flight crew. They sit in the cockpit and fly the plane, using instruments to make sure that the plane travels at the right speed and height.

cockpit

Passenger plane

This huge aeroplane is called a Jumbo jet. It carries up to 500 passengers at a time and flies long distances all over the world.

Four powerful jet engines are fixed under the Jumbo's wings.

Into space

We live on a planet called Earth. The Earth is surrounded by a layer of air called the atmosphere. Beyond the atmosphere is a vast space, containing the Sun, the Moon, and the other planets and stars. Astronauts in spacecraft can go out into this space to explore.

Solar system

The Earth is one of nine planets that move round the Sun in paths called orbits. The Sun and the nine planets are part of the solar system.

Neptune · Pluto · Uranus · Saturn · Earth · Mercury · Jupiter · Mars · Venus · Sun

Space shuttle

Early spacecraft were rockets that could only be used once. The space shuttle is special; it can be used many times. It has wings that help it to glide back to Earth.

fuel tank

The solid rocket boosters help to launch the shuttle into space.

Watching the stars

Stars are balls of very hot gas. On a clear night, we can see up to 2,500 stars in the sky. Scientists, called astronomers, work in observatories with giant telescopes to study the stars.

Satellites orbit the Earth, beaming down messages to special receivers called satellite dishes.

satellite

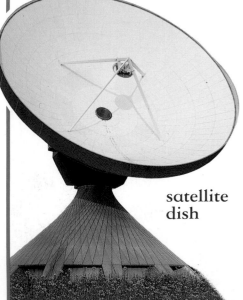

satellite dish

Satellite

Satellites are launched into space by rockets and space shuttles. They are used for forecasting weather, space research, and for beaming down television programmes.

USA

Discovery

Shuttle flight

Lifting off
The shuttle is launched. When it is 45km from the Earth, the boosters fall off and parachute into the sea.

Travelling in space
The shuttle rides into space on a large fuel tank. When the tank is used up, it falls back into the atmosphere.

Working in space
Once the shuttle is in orbit, the astronauts can start work. Their main job is to launch and repair satellites.

Space suit
When astronauts leave their spacecraft they wear space suits. Big backpacks are built into the suits to carry the oxygen the astronauts need to breathe.

The backpacks on the space suits also pump water through tubes in the astronauts' underwear to keep them cool.

In space, liquids do not pour. Astronauts have to suck their drinks from special tubes.

Weightlessness
When a spacecraft is in orbit, the people and things inside have no weight. They float in mid-air unless they are tied down. Astronauts sleep in special bags attached to the walls.

There is no wind on the Moon. The *Apollo* astronauts used a flag with a rod in it to make the flag stand out from its pole.

Moon landing
On 21 July 1969, two American astronauts were the first people to walk on the surface of the Moon. They travelled to the Moon in a huge rocket called *Apollo*. There have been five more Moon landings since then.

73

Index

A pronunciation guide to more difficult words is included in the index.

Acknowledgements

Dorling Kindersley would like to thank the following people
for their assistance in the production of this book:

Jacket design Karen Lieberman
Additional design Sharon Peters and Cheryl Tefler
Additional illustrations Janos Marffy
Picture research Catherine O'Rourke
Index Lyn Bresler

Picture Agency Credits

t=top; b=bottom; l=left; r=right; c=centre
Bruce Coleman Ltd/Gerald Cubitt 58 cr.
EPR Architects Ltd 32 tr, c, bl, 33 cl.
Robert Harding Picture Library 68 cr.
Oxford Scientific Films/TS McCann 64 br.
Science Photo Library/Tony Craddock 72bl;/
John Mead 72c;/NASA 72br, 73br.
Zefa 65 b.

Additional Photography

Simon Battensby, Paul Bricknell, Jane Burton, Peter Chadwick,
Andy Crawford, Geoff Dann, Philip Dowell, Michael Dunning,
Andreas Einsiedel, Philip Gatward, Steve Gorton, Frank Greenaway,
Stephen Hayward, Colin Keates, Dave King, Cyril Laubscher,
Dominic Marsden, Andrew McRobb, Ray Moller, Ian O' Leary,
Oxford Scientific Films, Stephen Oliver, Daniel Pangbourne,
Michael Pitts, Tim Ridley, Tim Shepherd/Oxford Scientific Films,
Karl Shone, James Stevenson/Greenwich Maritime Museum,
Kim Taylor, and Jerry Young.

Models

Dorling Kindersley would like to thank the following people
who appeared in this book:
Stacey Afrakumah, Rowena Alsey, Jodie Attreed, Heidi Barnes,
Jacob Brubert, Esther Bruml, Liza Bruml, Peter Bruml, Sarah Bruml,
Marion Burns, Simona Businaro, Lotte Butler, Hannah Capleton,
Gemmel Cole, Bobby Cooper, Matthew Cooper, Emma Cypress,
Sharon Daley-Johnson, Natalie Davidson, Liam Doyle, Mandy Earey,
Nicole Gabriel, Renee Gachette, Daniel Gregory, Dominic Harrison,
Paul Holden, Junji Hoshika, Naoko Hoshika, Miranda Hutcheon,
Andraé Johnson, Minhazel Kadir, Rebecca Kern, Gemma Loke,
Stella Love, Rachel Malicki, Brian Meggs, Nicci Meynell, Robert Nagle,
Paul Oakley, Hiral Patel, Howard Pedro, Sharon Peters,
Peter Radcliffe, Maxwell Ralph, Tebedge Ricketts, Audrey Roberts,
Peter Roberts, Simon Roberts, Stacey Ryan, Floyd Sayers,
Christian Sévigny, Amy Sherman, Kenji Shimizu, Natasha Singh,
Francis Taylor, Nicola Tuxworth, Melanie Voice, John Walden,
Lionel Wolovitz, Jane Yong, and Jane Yorke.

Additional Acknowledgements

Siobhan Power, Lesley Burke, Kerenza Harries, Julia Fletcher,
Snow and Rock, Pages Catering Supplies, Covent Garden Cycles,
Basketball Supply Company, World of Sport, Niels Montanana,
Mr FP McFerran of the London Judo Club, Toni and Guy
Academy, Franklin Delano Roosevelt School, John M Walker,
Philippines Department of Tourism, Ghana High Commission,
Audience Planners, Kew Gardens Palm House, Jenny Raworth,
Kentish Town City Farm, Start-rite Shoes, Keith Hoshika, and
Dawn Wiltshire of EPR Architects.